Belonging

three generations

Belonging

three generations

Poems by

Wendy Hoffman

© 2023 Wendy Hoffman. All rights reserved.
This material may not be reproduced in any form, published,
reprinted, recorded, performed, broadcast,
rewritten or redistributed without
the explicit permission of Wendy Hoffman.
All such actions are strictly prohibited by law.

Cover photo by Mae Mu
Cover design by Shay Culligan

ISBN: 978-1-63980-378-1

Kelsay Books
502 South 1040 East, A-119
American Fork, Utah 84003
Kelsaybooks.com

Acknowledgments

I thank Baron Wormser for his expert help with these poems and wise guidance, and Linda Convoy and Eugenie Simpson for their astute comments and steady support.

Contents

Foreword	13
Part I Bella	
Grandmothers	17
Bella	18
Bone Broth	19
History from Her Grandchild	20
What War Did	21
The First Hour of Their Day	22
The Choice	23
Whitman's Samplers	
on the Dining Room Table	
Forest Hills, 1940s	24
Husbands	25
Anniversary	27
The Corner Drugstore c. 1950	28
A Message from My Generation to Hers	29
Ancestors	30
Lives of Countries and Women	31
The Card Game	32
Her Kitchen Table	33
Her Eyes	34
Kitchen Sink	36
Presences	37
Horses	39
Part II Pearly	
Symbiosis	43
Childhood Summers	44
The Lid	45
Dark Doll	46
Slap	47

My Public Life as a Piano	49
The Clench	51
Cinderella	52
He Called Her a Nymphomaniac	53
Honeymoon	54
Their Ship	55
Movies	56
Family History	57
The Gift	58
Reprieve	59
White Lie	61
Last Chance	62
The Difference Between Their Generations	63

Part III Better Times

Better Times	67
Memorial	68
Jones Beach	69

Foreword

my ancestors died silent
strapped shut

there's my grandmother sixty years in her coffin
her rugged hands still rolling out strudel dough

and my mother always striving
wanting long after it ended

they latch onto my living body
saddle my swelling hump

echo my story
I whom

they did not find fetching
untwist

their tangled thoughts

fate loves tricks

Part I

Bella

Grandmothers

My family lived clustered: one up the hill, one down the hill, one a ten-minute drive away—a compromise because that husband wouldn't reside too close. We lived like that until the main one, Grandma, who came here out of necessity, died. Then she no longer raced down the hill, across the street and halfway up a hill, schlepping a too heavy bag, and we no longer found home cooked delicacies in our fridge. No more strudels, cheese cakes made with sour cream, pot and farmer cheeses, polichita, farfel, knockle, blintzes, beef or chicken krepler.

My family's vinegar-love marinated into from-scratch dough.

She had not taught her daughters these memorized recipes from the Old Country but reigned in her exclusive domain of kitchen-food.

I don't know who taught her, because she was from the generation who did not talk about their lives, and I from the one that did not know to ask and record.

Bella

I lie down to fall asleep and sometimes my heart becomes a cage full of birds, their wings throbbing, trying to fly out and away. The feeling takes me back over seven steep decades to my childhood bed with maple head and foot boards and my grandmother Bella pushing on the hard mattress, making it go up and down as she sang "Ah, ah baby" over and over. It calmed my flapping heart. It was just a moment, a gesture that reached into my prison. Immigrants had all sorts of tricks. Such moments hang in the air shining like freshly cut diamonds, all its facets glistening, indestructible. I reach out my hand.

She had to leave Belarus, like all the Jews. Their hearts became a tribe of terrorized birds looking to flee loved homes. How hard they had to work to be calm, hold on.

The up and down lulled me from the early bedroom, my mattress molded to faceted clouds, as leaping birds in my heart dreamed to her "ah, ah."

Bone Broth

Even overwork could not open the door to Bella's cage.

I pick bits of chicken off roasted bones that I use for bone broth.

And there is my grandmother, dead sixty years, who never knew
I reached adulthood much less old age—she is here in her full
apron at my kitchen table in this cramped room helping me
pull meat off a carcass and strip bones clean.

After her Thanksgiving feasts for her daughters, their
husbands and two children each, after they left and with dishes
put to rest, she'd sit at her own oval table and glean the large
turkey carcass. She loved its *tuchis,* allowed herself this
luxury that no one else would even want to touch—a treat
to herself for giving up desires, other talents while
working herself to an early death for family, for living
in the wrong time and place.

History from Her Grandchild

They escaped from the Old Country.
She arrived with her left-behind-
mother's wooden board, rolling pin
and her own husband. She and he
were children-just-turned-teenagers,
not literate in English. She passive,
he ambitious, she a giver, he a taker.

People show love in different ways.
Hers came from baking.
Her hands always moved seeking work.
Strudels kept her family in one piece
an ocean away from roots.

She'd bend over the floured board and roll
dough so thin her stubby fingers and clipped
nails shone through. A magician, she moved
the dough to the pan in one swoop. She dropped
slices of McIntosh apples, cinnamon, oil in
a long string bean line, cracked jagged shells,
ground and sprinkled walnut bits. Days before
she boiled marmalade and now spread it over
this filling. She rolled the stuffed dough round
and round, cocooning the insides from 350
degree heat.

For all her skill and ingenuity, like me, she could
not protect her children or grandchildren from him
and another world of hate.

What War Did

They kneaded and let rise
punched down and let rise again
these East European matriarchs
who ran the shops, birthed many children.
Their legacy was sour starters, *roshtshine*.

My mother's younger sisters sat
close together at a restaurant's
round table—one was visiting
from California, the other
still lived on Long Island.

"What kind of bread?" the waitress said
in a tired uniform.
My aunts giggled, then laughed
flinging themselves back in their chairs.
"Wonder bread," they harmonized.

Did I hear brewed resentment
to their history in that laughter
or was it post-immigrant relief?

Only the granddaughter bakes
heavy bread.
If her sluggish dough doesn't rise,
she encourages it in a steamy microwave.

The First Hour of Their Day

With her right hand and her number two pencil on a pad of white paper or used envelopes, she scribbled sharp pointed daisies in a steady circle, an endless loop of fear and dread as her husband Max droned in the background how the phone is for convenience and not conversation—(it was the 1940s when each call costs 10 cents for three minutes) but she did not hang up the black receiver

because Mother in her own apartment sat obediently in stone in the chair under the wall telephone with her other hand empty, listening and agreeing, tied by cool wires running in the air to her mother's apartment building, wires that bound them less strongly than the pull of their seamless hearts wrought over silent destinies while I crashed pans onto the green linoleum wishing I had a phone and a mother.

The Choice

My mother, Pearl, could spot beauty across a store,
though untrained, uneducated,
she had the eye and knew it.
Her mother didn't and didn't know it
but she knew enough to want
what Pearl had.

They shopped together mostly
on Queens Boulevard and the bargain
Klein's on 14th Street.
Mother would make a beeline for the best
and Bella buzzing would snatch it from her hands
with the stinging squeal of "I love it."

Why do desolate mothers usurp
from their daughters?
Long taught to have no rights,
Mother yielded always.
Yet she needed a loveliness like jewelry
to fill that gnawing ugly void.

Whitman's Samplers
on the Dining Room Table
Forest Hills, 1940s

When we had company, my father passed around boxes
of Whitman's candy. Some chocolates were solid, some
filled with flavored goo.
Men descended their long fingers, picked them out and left
the little paper cups which sighed as
the Samplers circulated.

He passed me around. From lap to bulging lap.
When I looked into the silent empty paper in the box that
preceded me, I thought that's what life is.

How to fill the cups? Walking, swimming, eating better
chocolate. Sunshine, shade.

Wives' giggles echoed from the other room,
the kitchen, as they gulped caramel, fudge, cherry and nut
filled pieces. My mother preferred caramel, my aunt cherry,
and my grandmother—almond coated chocolates.

Diminutive paper cups rattled with nothingness.
Old now, I still prefer the solid.

Husbands

Male and female noise converged, separated,
found one another, pulled apart and serenaded
membranes of our dreams.

High pitched ice cubes clinked endlessly against glasses
of ginger ale in the kitchen—male deep shouts
spread their smacking blue feathers in the adjacent room.

Marlene and I were asleep in the large bedroom,
the men gathered in the living room with the wives
squeezed around the refrigerator.

Males fighting to preside spread out on chairs.
These husbands knew all about the economy, politics,
which candidate to vote for and the world's future.

With their index fingers piercing the recoiled air,
their prophecies poured from wet mouths faster
than Cassandra could have blinked.

Tomorrow wives will have to sew buttons back
on their shirts around the chests of verbose men,
these proud Caesars of Queens, New York.

Their proclamations flew to the ceiling, wrestled
with ones already there.
Tangled and always shifting, they scratched, bit

and dangled from the chandelier as only those
of relatives can do. This ceiling contest reflected
the floor battle and ripped our nightmares.

After the men exhausted international problems,
they segued to the hair on their scalps and
how they weren't bald yet. Ironically, the oldest won.

The females kept serving those scraping glasses
as Marlene and I dreamed about being protected
but knew we would never be.

Anniversary

It takes dying to be real, finally.

My mother died on the same day she married six decades earlier

the same day they murdered
Martin Luther King.

She chose that very time to die
to tell her marriage killed her
though her own father may have had a lot to do with it.

My grandmother, whose eyes always shifted to the side
because she could not bear to know what presented plain as day,

would smile through chipped teeth, wore a bright chiffon
dress to her daughter's spring wedding.
Bridesmaids wore satin taffeta.

The Corner Drugstore c. 1950

Bella in her forties, considered old then, pushed
open the heavy door to the drug store on the corner
of Queens Boulevard and 68th Road. She pulled out
her penny and plunged it in the greasy slot. The dial
wavered like an inebriated head, didn't rise far enough
despite my corrective oxfords weighing at least two
pounds. I slouched.

In the store's glaring light, we strolled past packages
lined up on shelves to the soda fountain in the back.
She ordered a vanilla malted and chocolate milk shake,
and I downed them fast, making musical notes with straws.
She frowned. My appetite could match my plump father's.
I swirled on the rotating seat, kicked the shining bar with my heels.

Behind this ice cream paradise stood displays of comics.
She bought the weekly "Archie" and "Little Lulu," treasures.
Then we walked down the street, across another boulevard
and up a block to where I lived. She told my mother
that I had not gained weight. No one talked about why.

A Message from My Generation to Hers

how could she have escaped
born to parents and the times
like skin's prison
enslaved to customs, amoralities

for this immigrant who cooked
and served meals
no divorce possible
only enslavement

didn't have a chance during that era
to extricate herself or her children
gulped food in her kitchen in the middle of the night
to smother her outrages sheltered in mesh nets

even in front of her grandchildren, she said out loud
"marriage is a coffin for women"
her uneducated soul having reached new philosophical heights
in the same moment her conscience shattered

when she wasn't distracted by those deep thoughts
or downtrodden, she boomed laughter
painted her nails startling pink
bleached her dark European hair
piled *tchotchkes* on her bureaus
played poker in smokey rooms.

Ancestors

Grandmother's face soaked like clothes
on wash day
at her father's funeral.
The early afternoon light turned into a rainbow.

A child, not understanding, I pelted her
with "Why? He beat you, your mother
and was stingy."

In a wintry voice she spoke as if from
a distance into an ancient well within herself:
"We cry for what might have been different."
She had a simple, peasant wisdom,
not my mother's intricate, intelligent mind.

I observe strangers who court this what-might-have-been.
They live far away in Asia or Africa, stand on half shells
or clouds, open their arms and fly.
Ships at the bottom of the ocean unfurl their riches onto rafts.
Stars sprinkle gold.
The moon smiles kindly and showers human love.
They give to their known families
what-might-have-been.
My face is dry.

Lives of Countries and Women

hold forms of imposed blindness.

"What you don't know won't hurt you,"
she mumbled to me, us, herself.
It must have been a saying from the Old
Country where she was born—

White Russia turned Soviet Union
turned Russia with its centuries
of rampant violence, propelling hatreds.

A fly buzzed around drawn curtains
until it was squashed.

This woman shoveled dirt
until awareness lived in a grave.
Illiterate about her own life,
she had shadow daughters
who didn't remember, didn't know,
tore their insides.

One granddaughter, with a Cassandra
tongue, scratched and dug, pinched
and cleaved, cleaned an apple off the ground,
found familial rapes, thefts, strangulations.
To countrymen, her words became
swords in stale air.

Peace that strides with blind amnesia
is different from the calming of knowledge,
but both radiate sulfurous wounds.

The Card Game

Bella taught me and cousin Karen Canasta.
I often won—beginner's luck as they say.
When I was close to the finish, Grams would say
out loud what she assumed was in my hand.

We didn't play for money, blood or trinkets
but Bella would release a gambler's
energy that resembled mania,
energy that invaded and couldn't be plugged

while intelligent Karen sat blank and statuesque
(they said she beat her head against the wall)
and I fell through the floor in a despair
that curdled in old age.

Her Kitchen Table

In her small apartment, we sat at the round table large enough for children and grandchildren, ate herring, sturgeon, bagels, cream cheese and lox. She baked sugar cookies and cheese cake for the children, *mohn* cookies and apple strudel for adults. Never having finished school and during that long boat ride carrying my mother in her fifteen year old womb, she still became a genius cook and baker. We relaxed in her warm kitchen and gorged on a feeling of belonging. The air was velvet, almost normal family-like, with only one eruption when an aunt flung her razor comment at my sister who was whining about a headache while eating heartily. Half this aunt's face crumpled into a sneer. Some take to stoicism, others don't. My sister and mother liked to complain.

Grandfather came home. The air turned to acid fast. We inched together to make room. He removed his immaculate top coat and hat, sat at the head of the crowded table. Ravenous, he consumed soup and meat, burped, announced it was under-cooked, folded his napkin exactly, stood up. We scurried into our coats, glanced back at her—

Her Eyes

The cradling slopes of Forest Hills rocked us.
My grandmother always walked fast as if
rushing to Continental Bank in time to receive
interest for that day, so she wouldn't
make her husband angry.
She sped in front of me, though
we were only headed to Queens Boulevard
to do grocery shopping.
I was twelve and she was fifty,
once slender as a ribbon, now squat
and square with face made up
so she wouldn't look like an East
European immigrant in New York.
Her terrified crystal blue eyes
shifted sideways, piercing,
forming a bridge to something else.

A man across the street on the boulevard
whistled, its sound sharp, startling.
He looked like the man who fixed her car.
She plowed forward in her flat shoes
below her swollen ankles.
He did it again.
"Grams, he's calling you."
In a low voice, a little bitter, sad, she answered
as if talking to an unknown part of herself,
"It's been a long time since anyone whistled at me."
Four years later, her heart whispered its swansong.

I remember seeing my mother in a coffin
but not her.

I remember the funeral with all the relatives
I'd never met, sheets covering mirrors
in the apartment,
her bad husband's wails
like whistles as he rocked himself.

Kitchen Sink

Sometimes she let me, a shadow, stand
beside her and help.
That day, we washed and dried dishes.
It was afternoon, so they must have been
from lunch or cooking.
A slippery one dropped from my heated fists.
She creased her forehead like scallops
but allowed me to continue.

I shattered another, both echoed on linoleum.
She pulled the towel away,
looked at me suspiciously through her glazed
farm-girl eyes, swept up the chips
with her simmering, resigned self.

Decades slipped by before I sterilized
burnt rage that shifted from her to him.

Presences

On a stack of carpets I sit in an enchanted land—a riot of pristine shapes, patterns, colors, textures. A customer holding herself tight notices a Chinese rug with gold center, blue border, calm and quiet.

"I think that's my grandmother's. I have goose bumps. Did you buy it in Texas?" she asks. Hovering, the Iranian shopkeeper says, "It's possible," and jumps to his files.

The woman whips out her cell phone and sends a picture to her mother.

"Does it have a butterfly and pagoda on one corner?" There's the butterfly with pink wings. The shopkeeper moves furniture. There's the pagoda, stately in beige and purples.

I feel my dead grandmother. She loved luscious Chinese carpets. She hovers as I bake her poppy seed cookies that she calls *mohns,* cheese and apple cakes. I roll the oil dough thin like old skin and patch tears with dabs of strong tea.

Nights, she ate what she baked, grew from size 4 to 14 from a bit of pleasure without a morsel of comfort. She wasn't a bad woman. I feel her judging my having wandered from family, how I didn't become an obedient breeder, domestic servant, slithered from its grip into a box of fears.

I knead sour cream into butter, eggs, flour, sugar to make cheesecake dough. The slippery sour cream reminds me of my grandmother's hungry spirit. It coats my twitching fingers. She comes closer, kind, menacing, grabs the rolling pin from my hands, tucks it under her arm, sits on it. She tries to harness me, gripping my mouth.

Something eggs her on. I roar. We wrestle, I twist my foot. The Iranian shopkeeper doesn't want to let go of his Moroccan wedding carpet. "It's the only one I have," he cries. I roll out the cheesecake dough, eat *mohn* cookies with my feet sunk into traditional rugs that poor children are forced to weave.

Some grandmothers do not leave. One rotates over
the cell phone tower and store. Mine wants to be home,
in me. Flying carpets, stretched dough, pagodas.

Horses

My grandparents frequented the Midway movie theatre on Queens Boulevard. My grandfather watched by snoring. This particular Saturday night, my grandmother touched by pre-world-war spirits, perhaps Eve or pre-creation ones, stirred in her broken seat for the first time. She rose, galloped home and served herself a cup of Tetley tea. As the doors closed, the usher woke Max. He tumbled home. Livid, he screamed at her, "You embarrassed me."

Those were my first walking steps.

My husband found the cereal box more interesting than me. He had a taste for restaurants, a desire I did not share but I obeyed. One particular breakfast, he sat across from me reading as usual. For a while, I read the side of the newspaper facing me that he held in the air above his bowed head until Bella's spirit joined hands with Eve's. I reared on my back legs, touched his newspaper and her movie screen with my front hooves, neighed and left. He didn't notice until the waiter brought the check. "You embarrassed me," he later huffed.

Those were my second steps.

Part II

Pearly

Symbiosis

Mother leans on two pillows in bed.
She reads a paperback novel
of unrequited love, twirling
a clump of her luscious hair.
Her index finger circles faster
faster.

I am five or eight spying on her
through open French doors.
She is my mother but we are not close.
We watch each other with alarm.
In a flash, anything could happen.

Seventy years pass and I am in bed.
My left fingers twist strands of my greying
hair to the rhythm of the words I read.
Somehow—an inherited gesture, an askance
gene, she has stepped into me again.

I am not happy to see her but why fight.
We are entwined, attuned.

Childhood Summers

On damp after-dinners, fathers who never wash dishes take their children across the street to the hilly lawn not yet overgrown with stale post-war apartment buildings. They give each of us a glass jar with a lid of punched holes and explain "If the fireflies have air, they'll live longer."

Delighted with our one-sided game, we lift the tin covers to trap moving lights—green, yellow, blue banners zigzagging in steel air. We squeal, "Look, I caught five;" "I have ten." In circular final dances, desperate for their former life, they plunge against glass walls held by the plundering fingers of entranced girls and boys. The grass recoils, the sky hollers, the universe tosses out anguish.

In the middle of the most raucous group, a short frozen girl, elbows pressed into ribs, stares at three in her jar. On the edges near the bushes, a boy in green shorts cries ashamed. He holds a jar with one lightning bug motionless on the bottom. Other children dash erratically trapping dozens. Men clap one another on their shoulders, backs, hoisting themselves on their flashy egos.

Our mothers finish with kitchen chores and mandatory calls to their mothers about heart conditions and breathing problems caused by secondhand smoke, then shuffle their feet in sloppy steps across the parched road to join celebrations of nightly massacres. Fathers engrossed in beetles do not notice their uncertain wives hanging back. Frowning, one wife arches in her blue house dress, grits her jaws as her husband stations himself too close to a woman.

The boy in green shorts turns his jar over, digs a hole with a Popsicle stick, buries his firefly behind the bushes. The frozen girl watches, takes the lid off her jar as her toes scrub the unclean earth.

The Lid

Father grabbed an empty jar, punched tiny holes in its lid, rushed
across the street to the vacant field, snared a peacock firefly who had
been cruising through spring air in its sensuous orange.

I peered into the glass,
saw purple shadows, grass,
daisies and Mother.
Her crazy wings crashed against walls,
screeching, roaring, desperate for escape
or something but always lidded,
sealed, born too soon in the clench
of wrong times.
Air dribbled out.

Dark Doll

My fair sister scrubbed my face and back
hard with Ivory soap and a brittle washcloth.

Calling Mother into the bathroom,
"Look," she said, "I made her shades lighter."

Our mother peered, shuffled away,
her head drooped

in dissatisfaction as steady as my pigment.
I felt like one of the dark dolls permanently

abandoned to the sale rack at FAO Schwartz
and remained in the warm sudsy water.

My bath grew restless, swirled, undulated, the tub
sprung wide wings, flew out the second story window,

settled on a ledge, spun me on a colorless balloon
faraway toward an eager town of refuge.

The rough washcloth shriveled on cement
below the window.

Slap

Windows plunged forward
ceilings collapsed, chairs and love seat levitated
the wall-to-wall hid in a corner

I told about the grandfather
I had to because I thought
next time I'd be killed

Her face became bones and teeth
red curls straightened, rose to
the chandelier as she slapped

My cheek still talks about its sting-
bruise, her left behind palm print
as Sister who never before protected

or told anything
but knew the danger
whispered "He did that to me too"

Mother flung herself before me as if
she were worshiping, "Will you ever
forgive me?" she cried to the air

My chest puffed with pleasure
for a moment forgetting that
she would never have believed me

What is asking for forgiveness?
Does begging make it about
the one who let it happen?

In the bathroom, she examined
her face in the mirror, the one
face that mattered

* * *

Next day, she changed the locks
banned him from our apartment
screamed at her shadowy husband

For the first time, Sister and I spied
the father crying—crying because he
wouldn't be able to see his father anymore

Next scalding morning, her sister-in-law
said he did that to all the children
in her neighborhood but not of course to her own

Mother walked in circles with locked legs
mouth hung open, ears red
her bathrobe winged loose

as she sizzled, foamed
alternated between blindness and sight
while I disappeared behind the worn love seat

My Public Life as a Piano

after Bruno Schulz

Our small baby grand piano is forced to look cared for and nourished, obey on command, make sounds like a queasy curtsy before a queen, and never ever echo the mumbling water outside over-washed windows that sigh without interruption. Wood polished to a high gloss, white and black keys finely tuned, lid standing tall, it takes up the corner of the grey living room under wide windows overlooking waterfalls that never cease murmuring dark secrets. Sitting erect on its hard matching bench, Mother emitting a false smile presses on keys that shiver in a querulous groan. The piano teacher grimaces and straightens his tie. Mr. Brown eventually fires us pupils. We haven't practiced enough or at all. Like me, our piano feels ashamed and victorious.

Alone, I leave my skin on the bench, shrink into roundness, sliver oozing organs down the closing lid, mumble to myself through sad windows that echo and harmonize with the waterfalls and I become the piano.

My white keys press down, like lowered eyes, my black ones pop up, like frown marks, the strings inside me vibrate and my outer material stands taut. Some nights, when the family is asleep in the apartment—I hear Father snoring—and swans and geese are asleep outside in the waterfalls—when all is quiet and no one is listening or watching, I let out a groan and wail that puncture the living room walls and no one hears. Fabulous.

What would happen if someone heard? The mother would smash my face and threaten to throw me out the window, but no one hears and my groans blend with the subdued murmuring of the waters, and my wail reaches the skies. I finally fall asleep and snore too.

It's a new day. I stretch my piano legs, flex my globes of feet, feel the sun shine through the sparkling windows, strum my strings. I look toward the future in my new identity singing the blues, spilling out melancholy, being myself with no interference, pressure, inhibitions.

Life is good no matter who plays you.

When the smooth knobs on my legs, sturdy and graceful, turn back into human feet prancing gaily up the walls, hanging dutifully from the cut crystal chandelier imported from Italy and in a weak moment, swinging, reaching heights. Ah, what bliss—to no longer be a musical instrument, offspring, to swing in the stagnant air of escape, remoteness.

Still wildly rocking, I break the four black legs of the piano bench. My skin falls to the grey carpet constantly vacuumed. I throw the wooden legs, along with the keys, out hazy wide windows smashing them; their pieces fall in and out of the raucous room. Docile wind and fearful birds in a flurry fly in. Mother takes a broom and tries to shoo them out, but lands on one of their wings and flies out herself over the rush of the waterfalls and into the sterling blue. There's Sister flying too. I haven't seen her for a long time. She crashes into Mother. So she was angry all these years. They rise together into the celestial black. I lose sight as they round the corner calling back secret melodies.

The Clench

When our mother breathed
into a mirror, she saw
my stunning sister smiling back.

Her magical vapor
spun an invisible fusion
entwining Sister wherever she went.

At college, Sister became too thin.
In our parents' house, she and I
sat at the yellow kitchen table.

Her plate remained empty.
A piece of golden pound cake radiated
nearby, shimmering in the afternoon sun.

"Mother wants me to eat that.
I want to, but I don't want
to do what she wants."

"I'll eat it," I said already salivating.
She spread her ringed hand over the slice.
"Then she'd think I ate it."

Never before had I heard her inward thinking.
Her brain lay on the table
next to the palatable dessert.

One day, a man gave Sister
a joint, and she brought it to Mother
who nodding tucked it in her drawer.

Cinderella

According to Pearl's fairy tale
my gorgeous sister could do no
wrong and my dark self
could do no right.
Alas.

But once upon a time at dinner
Marlene refused to eat her
mashed potatoes.
Mother had mixed in chunks of steamed carrots.
"They look like they have measles," Marlene said.

Here was her budding poetic self sobbing out at the family table.
Her words flew over our lawyer-father preoccupied with the next
high-risk gamble. I laughed cheerily at the good joke, but
Mother's stifled creativity puffed up. She ordered cherished
Marlene to depart from the room without eating.
"Begone."

Mother must have thought she had created a vegetarian
masterpiece. Little did she know that she scolded a future writer,
nor suspect that in her own post-diagnosis years she would finally
write or that the despised daughter would follow their path.
The shoe would fit us all.
Genes.

What echoing ancestral voices
have been lost along the way—
how many unheard sleeping beauties
did not live happily ever after?
Farewell.

He Called Her a Nymphomaniac

I tried to peel a yellow banana splotched with green.
It didn't want to let go.
In my seventies, sympathy hit me.

In the 1940s, when she was young, my mother
watched a Florida tree unfurl a stalk of bananas.
Shaking in sad frustration,

she cried to the heavens
"Why not me, why not me?"
as leaves descended to fertile ground.

She often described the man
she should have married, someone in lingerie.
Her skin was soft with a natural fragrance.

Then how did women married to frigid
or absent men not shatter?
Hers was a pedophile.

Mother hummed when she darted dark
ocean waves, moaned when floating
on intoxicating lakes, groaned when the juice

of voluptuous peaches meandered down her arms,
was ecstatic when she neared lilacs.
She sucked on mango pits.

I tug the peel off the reluctant banana.
The over ripe inside does not match
its tough exterior.

Honeymoon

Our parents gave my sister a lingerie trousseau from Bergdorf's.
The eager nightgowns hung high on an open rack like an altar
in their laundry room. Mother would linger, rippling pastel
satins, silks, lace trims, exuberant puffs of embroidered petals.

Her cheeks and chin reddened as she strayed to fantasies
of being carried away, ravaged, adored after her own wedding.
She became twenty again when life had not yet engraved
her face with disappointment, bitten her expectant spine,

heightened her awareness of peers who started out
with less and ended up with everything.
She'd caress her daughter's marital materials,
drain her bleeding cavern of squeezed hopes.

Their Ship

Her husband was a gambler.
If money piled in his pocket,
he'd throw it on the next best bet.

We read in the Times that he lost $60,000
a fortune then
on Batman Tee shirts.

Mother said he became hooked
when older boys let him win at poker.
His oily charm endeared his victims.

She'd stroll aimlessly, rush haphazardly
around the cramped apartment
sighing, "When our ship comes in."

On his way to play chronic golf
he'd echo, "When my ship comes in,"
his breath covering mirrors.

She endured her hungry 20s, 30s, grasping 40s, 50s
when divorcing him staggered relatives.
She became a new kind of pioneer.

For another decade, Pearl's salmon-like heart
backstroked upstream.
Her daughters swam with her hard-won bet.

Movies

We sat in the gaudy movie theater where the family went maybe once a month, especially if a Hitchcock played and on Christmas and New Year's. I stood behind my mother so that I could finger the soft lobe of her ear just the way my grandmother would meld oil dough for her strudels, long and thin like eels before they came out of the oven brown and tender like me. I was born dark like her father and therefore Mother hated me.

She sat frozen in front of me in the red velvet upholstered seat smelling like popcorn. She took off her diamond earrings before we left the apartment and let me mold her ear lobe over and over as I strove for a comfort connection and she, long suffering, a reprieve. She must have thought this sacrifice would buy her time to watch the show in peace.

Years later, after we moved to Long Island, we didn't go to the movies together. Still fingers in my mind forge a false connection as my dead grandmother stretches her strudel dough without a tear or hole.

Family History

"A woman is no better than the man she marries," Bella would say
over her cup of tea, sweetened by a drop of honey, soured by
a lemon slice and over a *lekvar** hamantachen placed on a
chipped plate. She meant the wife had to be an accomplice.

Her daughter, my mother, severed this decree by divorcing.
(*A cancer diagnosis makes people realize.*)
No matter that she regretted it later. She still did it.
Out of his grip, she concluded
"A man just wants a friendly cook."

I followed the lead but lacked her ingenuity, waited
until he wanted the separation.
Afterward I said
"Now I can live."

My older sister followed on her own
but her breadwinner was a seething alcoholic.
Mother consoled her with
"There are many paths and you have your own."

Mother and her daughters signaled
there is another planet rotating in the shining
hemispheres where downtrodden slaves who cook
goulashes do not live.

* prune butter

The Gift

After she'd lost hope that he'd return,
after the concentric growth on her tumid nipple
pulsed and bled—she called it an octopus—
at the tip of her blanched life—

after all that—my sister gave her a blank notebook.
That's how Pearly found herself, right before it was too late.
She wrote her stories at Overeaters Anonymous meetings.
(Even though she was emaciated, she had become fat

during pregnancy.) There she spread her wisdom
like luxurious wings, an icon for the mother-deprived.
Four hundred of these sensitive friends would attend
her funeral and later publish her stringent sayings.

All her astringent life, she'd see backbreaking beauty
in a bush as she walked along the street or in tumultuous
skies or a dancer's arms as she watched TV or in the scent of color.
Now she spewed her life on paper, not her deepest, not the one

around the bone though she came miraculously close,
but the truth of the outward one that she was permitted to know.
With her ballpoint and a stack of filled miscellaneous notebooks,
she ceased yearning for her desired enemy.

Reprieve

She wasn't ready for Death and fenced.
Her ex-husband sent her to a Mexican clinic

where she ingested ground apricot pits, a Laetrile treatment.
Her hair and nails fell off as if to flee a betrayed body.

Under a cool sun, the sick luxuriated in imagined safety,
in unity fought the shared impartial enemy

while blind to a new thief that seized their bloodstreams
through narrowed veins

and new assailants who profited
from their innocence.

The patients exchanged rings of melted silver spoons.
Hers reached beyond her finger's second joint.

She felt safe, belonged for the first time,
changed her name from Pearl to Pearly

returned to her barricaded tunnel, barely furnished
Bronx apartment, the family she did not love.

Breast cancer brought her communion among fellow patients,
sent her to writing groups, for the first time.

After all her life's tedious domestic tasks, under the housewife,
she discovered a writer.

The peril of talent is to deny it and the self.
The smoothed oyster's pearl forced her false selves to flee.

Wind blew through shivering rooms, drapes
darkened, a black cloak roamed narrow passages.

Death stalked her
until both shrieking it took her.

White Lie

One of the last times I saw my mother, she was thin, tense, bent over and wore all black. Air in her studio apartment seemed stagnant, layered with musty loneliness, isolation. The ill know those enclosures. She offered me store-bought cookies that she took from her freezer and defrosted. They were far from what she used to take pleasure in serving—a butter dough dipped in egg and ground sugared walnuts, baked until golden. A Hungarian recipe. When she went to the bathroom, I pretended to eat one of the stale cookies. She peered into the yellow plate. "It doesn't look like you ate any," she said. I lied again. Can you trick someone you love even with a white lie? She frowned and looked into the distance and inward. I spent most of my life knowing the truth and being told something else. My sister arrived, a relief to us.

I left soon after. Mother died two years later. I felt a black hole center in my heart and a new kind of hollowness for what might have been.

Last Chance

Since the diagnosis, she allowed herself
only raw vegetables, fruits and nuts.

She wanted one of her green drinks
and told me how to blend it.

When I combined her ingredients, the color looked wrong.
Too much kale. I altered it,

delivered the drink to her hospital bed.
In the past, she had accused me of being high-handed.

She sipped and grimaced.
"I know what I'm doing," she said.

The dying can have Herculean strength of a kind.
Through the ending haze,

her hazel eyes, long glistening swords,
pierced me sideways.

I had failed my last chance.
Afterward, I felt an ancient yearning

as for an organ peeled away
without love.

The Difference Between Their Generations

is cans of soup
as in Warhol's paintings/posters.
Freedom for one became convenience for the other.

Grandmother knew she lived in America
because she was not a soldier's widow
or a beaten prostitute.

Mother knew because of Campbell's Tomato Soup.
Lunchtimes she would get out her can opener and twist.
Sometimes she added saltines.
Manufactured products, the new religion.
Stove fans combed away the preservative smell.

Grandma with taste buds that remained in East Europe
simmered chicken bones. Mother steamed vegetables
while Grams added giant lima beans to her heavy broths
whose aroma bubbled through her apartment building
tantalizing bachelors who'd lift their heads to sniff.

But both packaged their formerly perfectly fine hair,
Grandma preferred Hollywood blonde,
Mother used Miss Clairol's' Sunberry.

Part III

Better Times

Better Times

Turkeys needed more time to roast then.
At 2:30 Thanksgiving mornings, Mother would stuff
a huge one with a Ritz cracker mixture,

Father would rise at 3:00, heat the oven to 250 degrees,
place the slaughtered bird inside.
Hardly any fights or disagreements occurred those days.

They worked as a team in early times
when the family was intact,
when parents matched TV families:

dancing grass was green and perky
sky blue with sunny clouds
air exuded spiced aromas
children laughed
dogs were quiet, cats purred.

We watched *Your Show of Shows* on TV, ate apple pie.
By 10 at night, Mother collapsed into bed,
Father washed the dishes and played Solitaire
until the more usual morrow.

Memorial

One afternoon every year, in snow or sun,
I watched her mold my chocolate layered birthday cake.

She reached onto the shelf lined with pink and green
oil cloth and frilly trim, pulled out Hershey's Cocoa Powder.

She mixed ingredients in her large yellow bowl,
adding buttermilk drop by sloppy drop.

Her long-fingered sugary hands rippled sweet smelling air.
After she beat heavy cream, added vanilla, I licked

the beaters, my tongue curling around their
slender cage-like bars.

Those times were my reprieve, peace,
a pat, moment of grace for her too,

when she turned into her self and showed
the earnest love that was stored in her cavernous soul

and ricocheting brain—before our lives
threw off their pink packaging and green covers.

Jones Beach

On the shores of Long Island
we made drip castles.
Knots of sand squeezed through
our sensual, eager fingers.
I liked to fill tin pails, pat them flat, turn
them upside down and spring fat castle walls
the way Grandmother released lemon cakes
from pans in her tiny kitchen of heavenly smells.

Untamed salty fish air swirled around
our darkening bodies, enclosed, absorbed.
Our bathing suits clung, scratched.
Older boys joined, our palaces grew into whole
communities like developments springing up
all over with split levels, ranch houses.
Until the tides buried them.

We gorged on green grapes as our spirits
faltered but did not suspect that unseen
currents molded, turned us upside
down, leaving mounds that
would drip onto our lives' hidden paths.

About the Author

Wendy Hoffman has published three memoirs, *The Enslaved Queen* (Karnac Books, 2014, new edition by Aeon Books, 2019), *White Witch in a Black Robe* (Karnac Books, 2016, new edition by Aeon Books, 2019) and *A Brain of My Own* (Aeon Books, 2020, Phoenix and Karnac Books, 2023). *The Enslaved Queen* has been translated and published in Germany (Asanger-Verlag, 2021). Her book of poetry, *Forceps,* was also published (Karnac Books, 2016), along with a book of essays, *From the Trenches,* written with Dr. Alison Miller (Karnac Books, 2018, re-issued Routledge Books, 2019, Pheonix and Karnac Books, 2023). Her fourth memoir, *After Amnesia*, is published on the SmartNews and Survivorship websites (2022). It also has been translated into German.

www.ingramcontent.com/pod-product-compliance
Lightning Source LLC
Chambersburg PA
CBHW030913170426
43193CB00009BA/837